GET HAPPY SERIES : RELATIONSHIPS AND COMMUNICATION

Workbook and Journal Prompts

Erin Vandermore

Stop & Breathe, Inc.

I want to dedicate this book to my loved ones who have supported me throughout my writing journey. To my wife, who has always been my sounding board, even when she's tired and just wants to unwind on her phone. To my daughter Emma, who has taught me the importance of patience and fun. To my son Alex, whose never-ending questions keep me on my toes. And to my furry companions, who remind me to take breaks from work, though I would appreciate it if they could stop digging holes in the backyard to get my attention. I'd also like to thank my siblings, Jack and Stevie, for allowing me to practice my conflict resolution skills as a child. Finally, I thank my parents, Steve and Val, who have always been there for me, and for whom I am grateful every night before I go to bed (an inside family joke).

CONTENTS

Title Page
Dedication
Introduction
Prologue
Relationships 1
Your Relationship with Yourself 7
A Funny Story About Karen 14
Exploring Love and Connection: 20
Love 56
many different types of love 60
why can't i make someone love me? 64
Stages of a Romantic Relationship 79
Boundaries 93
What is the importance of enforcing boundaries? 98
Why 101
Connection 105
Relationships with Kiddos 120
Parenting Styles & their Impact 122
Attachment 127
I'm already an Adult; is it too late for me? 132
So it's all my parent's fault 134

Communication	**146**
General Types of communication:	**152**
Setting Ground Rules for Communication	**161**
Active listening	**166**
Rules to Fight Fair	**177**
Story Time	**195**
WTF is the 100% Rule?	**197**
Story Time	**200**
Epilogue	**215**
Afterword	**219**
About The Author	**223**

INTRODUCTION

A healthy relationship is one where two or morepeople treat each other with respect and kindness. Both parties should communicate their thoughts and feelings openly, honestly, and without fear of judgment. They should also support each other in making decisions that are best for them both. Healthy relationships are based on trust, acceptance, and understanding, all of which lead to a robust and lasting connection. Finally, healthy relationships are built on mutual respect, so everyone involved should be willing to compromise and work together for the benefit of the relationship.

PROLOGUE

As a therapist, I avoided giving advice when I started; it's considered a "no-no" and not viewed in the best light within the field. Also, it's stronger at times and more important to come to self-realization when possible. However, we humans are constantly seeking advice, so why would I not give you any and send you to your biased friends instead? We all have our judgments and biases, but as a therapist, well, first, I don't know you or have any preconceived notions about you or your life. I can provide that unbiased view that your friends and family can't, not because they don't want to but because they are influenced by their opinions and love for you; they want to protect your feelings. So, I started to give my view on situations. However, only some have the privilege to have a therapist. Also, in the 21st century, mental health is still taboo, and some are without insurance or prioritize other areas in their lives; whatever the reason might be, we as a society are not working on preventative care for our mental health. I especially felt and saw this as a mental health therapist who lived through COVID; during my "downtime" working remotely, running a household, and helping two children in children in two separate schools navigate remote learning. I wanted help, knowing that years after COVID, our mental health will suffer while no longer having the spotlight that COVID provided. I wanted to give back and share what I could- hence a series of books. I'm not using my knowledge as a therapist to persuade anyone to receive any treatment they are not ready for; simply to suggest a proposal, an idea around the idea of working on yourself, increasing your ability to express yourself, and understand yourself and live a happier life. Let's start working towards understanding ourselves and what does and does not make us happy.

The Get Happy series is designed for anyone interested in starting to work towards greater happiness in their lives. For over the past 10 years as a mental health therapist, I've noticed that specific themes come up over and over again. No matter your gender, race, or age, these issues are universal- for example, how to get along better with your in-laws or increase your self-esteem. So, this series includes journals and workbook pages to help you get happy with yourself and your life. I try to keep all the books in my series short, direct, and to the point. I do this for a couple of reasons; first, I have a short attention span, and second, being from Chicago, I don't particularly appreciate wasting time. I try to provide my readers with a no-nonsense approach that is simple and easy to do; creating new patterns is hard as hell, and if we want to be successful, we need to make it as simple as possible. I touch on many different topics and do not dive in deep; it's an introduction to many issues that are brought up within therapy sessions, coaching sessions, and homes throughout the country. It's the perfect way to start your journey towards happiness.

So, let's get started!

RELATIONSHIPS

Relationships are the best! And unfortunately, sometimes they are the worse. They provide us with so many incredible benefits, like having friends to share our lives with and people who can be there for us when things get tough. We get to enjoy the laughs that come along with a relationship. Nothing can bring more joy than being surrounded by the people we care about. Having relationships in our lives makes us happier and more fulfilled. Plus, it's always great to have someone to talk to when you need advice or want someone to listen.

Without relationships, we would be missing out on so much! We wouldn't have that special bond with someone that only comes from being close to them. We wouldn't get to experience all the love, joy, and laughter that come with healthy relationships. Relationships are one of the most essential parts of life and a great way to stay connected and happy. We all know that relationships can be hard work, but it's worth it in the end.

Putting effort into your relationships keeps them strong and ensures everyone involved feels cared for and respected. It takes communication, compromise, and a willingness to understand each other. We all crave connection with other people, even if it's just talking to a volleyball, like in that movie! Healthy romantic, platonic, or familial relationships can make life so much better. They provide us with essential emotional and physical support — it's why we strive for them to be healthy.

And even though it can be a challenge sometimes, the rewards of having close relationships in your life make it all worth it. Having multiple types of relationships is a great way to stay happy and healthy. Don't just rely on one connection — have friends, companions, and acquaintances with different kinds of people from different backgrounds. It could be a close friend, a family member, or even someone you talk to now and then. That way, you'll have many people to help support you and your well-being. It also helps to take off the pressure of a romantic relationship by being responsible for everything you need from just one relationship.

There are many ways that someone can put the effort into a relationship.

Here are five quick suggestions:

1. **Communication:** Regular, open, and honest communication is the foundation of any healthy relationship. Make time to talk to the other person, and practice active listening to fully understand their perspective.

2. **Quality Time:** Spend time with the other person doing things you both enjoy. Make time for dates or outings that allow you to connect and bond with each other.

3. **Support:** Support the other person emotionally and mentally and show interest in their passions and hobbies. Be there for them during challenging times and celebrate their successes.

4. **Compromise and Negotiation**: Not every decision will be easy, but it's crucial to participate in honest and open dialogue to come to a solution that works for both people.

5. **Acts of Service:** Show the other person that they are essential to you by doing things for them. This could be a simple gesture, such as bringing them coffee, or something more significant such as helping them with a project they're working on.

Remember that each relationship is different, and it's essential to communicate with the other person to understand what they need and want out of the relationship. By doing so, you can work together to create a strong and lasting connection.

A common myth about marriage is that if you have someone who loves you deeply and without conditions, you don't need any love from anyone else. Unfortunately, this misconception has been the cause of heartache for lots of couples. Marriage, Partnership can be great - it can make us happy, help us grow, challenge us in all the right ways, and keep life fun- but it's an illusion to believe that this one relationship is all you need. To be content, we need friends, a job that makes us happy, some alone time, fun activities, and other experiences. Unrealistic expectations will only lead to letdowns.

A healthy relationship is characterized by mutual respect, trust, openness, support, communication, and shared responsibility. On the other hand, an unhealthy relationship is marked by abuse, manipulation, lack of communication, disrespect, power imbalances, and infidelity. Here are some specific examples:

Signs of a Healthy Relationship:

- Both partners have equal say and decision- making power in the relationship.

- Everyone feels secure and respected, and there is mutual trust and honesty.

- Communication is open, honest, and non-judgmental.

- Both partners are supportive of each other's goals and aspirations.

- There is a healthy balance between independence and interdependence.
- Conflicts are resolved respectfully and constructively.

Signs of an Unhealthy Relationship:

- One partner dominates the other, making most decisions and controlling the relationship.
- Lying, deception, and dishonesty are common.
- Communication is minimal, vague, or insincere, leading to misunderstandings and tension.
- One partner berates, criticizes, or belittles the other regularly.
- One partner displays aggressive or violent behavior, causing fear and physical harm to the other.
- Infidelity or emotional affairs occur.

It's important to remember that relationships can be complex and nuanced, and it's often not as simple as "healthy" or "unhealthy." However, understanding what behaviors and attitudes contribute to a healthy relationship can help individuals cultivate solid and fulfilling connections with others while avoiding the pitfalls of unhealthy ones.

Realizing that one person cannot meet all your emotional needs can be upsetting because human emotions are complex and multifaceted. No single person can embody every emotion or respond to every emotional need similarly. We each have different personalities, experiences, and coping mechanisms, which affect our emotional responses.

Additionally, relying too heavily on one person for emotional support can create a power imbalance and put undue pressure on the relationship. Accepting that multiple connections may be necessary to fulfill our emotional needs can be challenging, but it ultimately allows for more diverse and balanced emotional support.

YOUR RELATIONSHIP WITH YOURSELF

It's essential to have a healthy relationship with yourself as well. When you're in tune with your needs and feelings, it can help stop selfish behavior. Instead of taking out your frustrations on others, you'll be better able to work through them by yourself or with someone else positively. A good self-relationship will allow you to live life confidently and free from unnecessary stress. Relationships are essential for our mental and physical health. Having strong connections with those around us can help reduce anxiety and depression and even improve our physical health in the long run. This is why nurturing and strengthening all your relationships — with yourself and those around you is so important. Having a healthy relationship with yourself can be challenging, but it is essential for creating meaningful relationships with others. Start by gaining insight into your values, beliefs, and needs to understand who you are and what matters to you most. From there, strive to make decisions that align with those values and take time each day to show yourself love and appreciation.

6 steps to get you started down the road of knowing yourself; to gain insight into your values, beliefs, and needs:

1. Reflect on Your Life: Consider the events, experiences, and relationships that have shaped you. Think about moments that have brought you joy, fulfillment, and satisfaction, as well as those that have caused discomfort, anxiety, or sadness.

2. Identify Important Relationships: Consider the people in your life who are most important to you and the role they play. Think about how they align or differ from your own beliefs and values.

3. Consider Your Goals: Think about what you would like to accomplish in life and the motivations behind those goals. Consider how your values align with your aspirations.

4. Write It Down: Put your thoughts down on paper by journaling or making lists. This can help you organize your thoughts and gain clarity on your values and beliefs.

5. Seek Feedback: Ask trusted friends, family members, or a therapist for feedback on your values and beliefs. This can help you gain an outside perspective on aspects of your character that may be hard to see.

6. Examine Your Behavior: Consider how your actions align with your values and beliefs. If there are discrepancies, think about why and how you can bring your behavior into better alignment with your values.

By using these strategies, you can develop a deeper understanding of who you are and what matters to you most, allowing you to make conscious choices and live a more fulfilling life.

Self-love is a topic that will either get me snickers or eye rolls, depending on the audience. In therapy sessions, when a client gives me a funny look and or will caustically say, "Sure," I'm not telling you to look into a mirror and gaze fondly at yourself for hours. I don't expect anyone to do daily affirmations with Stuart Smalley and say, "I'm Good Enough, I'm Smart Enough, and Doggone It, People Like Me!" while looking in the mirror. But if that makes you laugh, then by all means, do it. The skit, although funny, unfortunately, made affirmations become comical when they were extremely powerful. Just think of all the negative thoughts you tell yourself all day long; pause if you need time to count. Now if you took that number and said that many positive affirmations to yourself every day- well, you first would never leave the mirror and, second, wouldn't need to read a book about increasing your happiness.

Additionally, practice self-compassion by acknowledging your mistakes without judgment or criticism. Learning how to accept yourself and be comfortable in your own skin is an essential step to forming successful relationships with those around you. Practicing self-compassion involves treating ourselves with kindness, understanding, and empathy.

Examples of Kind vs. Unkind Self-Talk

Kind Self-Talk:

"I am proud of my accomplishments and the progress I've made."

"I am doing my best, and that's enough."

"I deserve love and respect from myself and others."

"I am strong and capable of overcoming challenges."

"It's okay to make mistakes; they are opportunities for growth."

Unkind Self-Talk:

"I'm not good enough."

"I always mess things up."

"Nobody likes or cares about me."

"I'll never be able to achieve my goals."

"I'm a failure."

These reflective journal prompts, will help you gain a deeper understanding of the relationship with yourself and how you speak about yourself. Cultivating kind self-talk and recognizing your worth will help you build a stronger, more positive connection with yourself.

Self-Talk Awareness: Reflect on a recent situation where you experienced self-doubt or faced a challenge. What kind of self-talk did you engage in? Was it kind or unkind? How did it impact your emotions and actions?

Positive Affirmations: Write down five positive affirmations about yourself, focusing on your strengths, abilities, and qualities. Practice repeating these affirmations daily to cultivate kinder self-talk.

Turning Negatives into Positives: Think about an unkind thought you've had about yourself recently. Rewrite it into a positive, encouraging statement. How does this shift in perspective affect your feelings and outlook?

Compassion and Forgiveness: Reflect on a time when you made a mistake or faced criticism. How did you speak to yourself during that situation? Consider how you would have treated a friend in the same situation. How can you show yourself the same compassion and forgiveness?

Celebrating Success: Write down three accomplishments or moments of personal growth you're proud of. How did you talk to yourself during those times? How can you continue to acknowledge and celebrate your successes?

A FUNNY STORY ABOUT KAREN

(not that type of Karen- poor Karens of the world who are nice and just happen to have that name)

Once upon a time, there was a woman named Karen who prided herself on being independent and self-sufficient. But secretly, Karen envied her friends who were in relationships and constantly posted cute couple pictures on social media.

One day, Karen decided to take matters into her own hands and create her own love story. So, she printed a picture of herself, drew a face on it, and placed it in a frame. She then took the image out to dinner and a movie. During the dinner, Karen found herself laughing and having a great time. At the movie, she held hands with the picture and whispered sweet nothings to it.

As Karen walked home with her picture, she couldn't help but feel a sense of satisfaction. She patted the frame and said, "Karen, you're a catch. Any person would be lucky to have you."

The next day, Karen proudly posted a picture of her and her date on social media with the caption, "Finally found the one!" Her friends were confused but congratulated her nonetheless.

From that day on, Karen continued to shower herself with love and affection, always remembering that the most crucial relationship in her life was the one with herself.

The moral of the story? You don't need another person in your life to find true love. The love you have for yourself is just as essential and can be just as satisfying. Plus, you don't have to share the popcorn!

Here are some ways to practice self-compassion:

o **Speak kindly to yourself:** Use compassionate language when speaking to yourself. Instead of harshly criticizing yourself, talk to yourself as you would to a friend in need.

o **Recognize your common humanity**: Remember that everyone experiences struggles and challenges, and you are no exception. Recognizing that you're not alone can help cultivate self-compassion.

o **Practice mindfulness:** Take time to be present in the moment and tune in to your thoughts and feelings. Mindfulness can help you develop greater awareness and non-judgmental acceptance of your experiences.

o **Validate your emotions:** Allow yourself to feel your emotions without judgment. Acknowledge your feelings and offer yourself comfort and support. (In the mirror if it makes you smile)

o **Practice self-care:** Engage in activities that bring you joy and relaxation. Show yourself the same care and attention you would to a loved one.

o   **Seek support:** Reach out to friends, family members, or a mental health professional for help and guidance.

Practicing self-compassion does not mean being self-indulgent or letting go of personal responsibility. Instead, it involves treating ourselves with the same kindness and support we would offer to others. By cultivating self-compassion, we can enhance our resilience, well-being, and overall satisfaction in life.

Establishing boundaries and expectations for yourself, just as you would in any other relationship, is essential. Have honest conversations with yourself about what these boundaries are and the consequences of breaking them. Practicing self-discipline is crucial in developing a positive relationship with yourself, and when done with kindness and respect, it will make you feel respected and seen.

A boundary and expectation for yourself might look like setting limits on how much time you spend engaging with other people. This could mean limiting the number of social activities you participate in or setting a time limit for interactions with others. Additionally, it could involve taking breaks from technology or limiting contact after certain hours. It is also essential to set boundaries concerning personal space and respect for others. For example, you might establish an expectation that people will treat you with respect and not invade your personal space without permission.

Setting boundaries also includes taking responsibility for yourself and understanding when it is time to take a step back from specific conversations or situations. It's important to establish expectations around emotional well-being and self-care. This could involve setting aside time for yourself to relax, practice mindfulness or engage in activities that bring you joy.

Establishing these boundaries and expectations will help ensure that your relationships are healthy, respectful, and meaningful. By setting clear rules of communication, understanding your values and needs, showing respect, and communicating openly, you can create positive and supportive relationships with yourself and those around you. Taking the time to practice these tips will help ensure that your relationships are successful and fulfilling.

Establishing a trusting relationship with yourself is vital to healthy relationships with others. Once you understand what matters most to you, it can help inform the types of relationships you want to cultivate. Being aware of boundaries is also essential, so it's important to know when someone may be crossing a line or not respecting your needs or wishes.

Establishing these boundaries and communicating them

effectively can help ensure that you are feeling respected and supported in all your relationships. Lastly, focus on being honest with yourself and others. This involves speaking your truth, even if it's uncomfortable, and having an open dialogue about expectations. When having this discussion, be sure to remain respectful and open-minded so that all parties involved can come to an agreement on what is acceptable. Doing this will ensure that everyone's needs are being respected while still fostering meaningful relationships.

Taking the time to practice these skills will help create healthy relationships between yourself and others, paving the way for successful communication. By taking time to reflect on your values, boundaries, and needs, you can foster meaningful relationships with yourself as well as other people.

EXPLORING LOVE AND CONNECTION:

REFLECTIVE JOURNAL PROMPTS TO ASSESS YOUR ROMANTIC RELATIONSHIP

By reflecting on these prompts, you'll gain a deeper understanding of the health of your romantic relationship. This will help you identify areas of strength and areas that may need attention, leading to a stronger, more fulfilling partnership.

Good Times and Challenges: Think about the happy moments and tough times in your relationship.

1. Write down three of your favorite memories and three challenging situations you've faced together.

MY NOTES

2. How did you both handle these situations?

MY NOTES

3. Did you feel supported and understood by your partner?

MY NOTES

MY NOTES

Communication Style: Reflect on how you and your partner communicate with each other.

MY NOTES

1. Are you honest, open, and respectful when discussing your feelings and thoughts?

MY NOTES

2. Write down a recent conversation where you felt heard and understood, and another where communication could have been better.

MY NOTES

Balancing Act: Consider the balance between giving and receiving in your relationship.
1. Do you both make an effort to support each other's needs, interests, and goals?

MY NOTES

2. List some examples of how your partner has shown support for you, and how you have supported them.

MY NOTES

3. Is there a healthy balance, or does one person give more than the other?

MY NOTES

MY NOTES

Quality Time: Think about the time you spend together as a couple. 1. Do you enjoy doing fun activities and sharing meaningful experiences?

MY NOTES

2. Write down your three favorite activities to do together and any new activities you'd like to try.

MY NOTES

3. What can you both do to improve your communication?

MY NOTES

MY NOTES

3. Are you both open to exploring new interests together?

MY NOTES

Here are the 8 main ingredients to create and maintain a healthy relationship:

1. **Communication:** Regular and open communication is the foundation of a healthy relationship. Make time to talk to your partner and practice active listening to fully understand their perspective. (Yes, communication again – I repeat because it's that important)

2. **Trust:** Building trust in a relationship takes time, but it's essential for it to thrive. Be honest and keep your promises to build trust with your partner.

3. **Respect:** Respect is a crucial factor in any healthy relationship. Respect your partner's opinions, boundaries, and thoughts. Treat your partner the way you want to be treated.

4. **Compromise:** Disagreements in healthy relationships are inevitable, but it's essential to find a middle ground. Try to work on finding common ground and make compromises while respecting each other's boundaries.

5. **Quality Time:** Spending time together is vital in maintaining a healthy relationship. Make time to go on dates or plan activities that you both enjoy.

6. **Support:** Supporting your partner in their goals,

dreams, and aspirations is essential. Show interest in their passions and hobbies, and be there for them during tough times.

7. **Physical Affection**: Physical affection, like holding hands or hugs, is essential in maintaining the emotional connection between couples.

8. **Gratitude:** Expressing gratitude towards your partner can strengthen the bonds between you two. Saying thank you or appreciating your partner can go a long way.

Remember, it's essential to communicate clearly and openly and ensure that both parties know what they want from the relationship. A healthy relationship can be developed and maintained with time, effort, and communication.

By exploring these reflective journal prompts, you'll gain a deeper understanding of the eight ingredients that contribute to a healthy, thriving relationship. This self-awareness will help you and your partner continue to grow and strengthen your relationship.

Communication Check-In: Reflect on a recent conversation with your partner where you felt truly heard and understood.

MY NOTES

What made that conversation successful?

MY NOTES

Now, consider a conversation where communication could have been improved. What steps can you take to enhance communication in your relationship?

MY NOTES

Building Trust: Write down three instances when your partner demonstrated trustworthiness, and three times when you showed trustworthiness to your partner.

MY NOTES

How do these actions contribute to the overall trust in your relationship?

MY NOTES

Respect Matters: Think about a situation where your partner showed respect for your opinions or boundaries. How did it make you feel?

MY NOTES

Conversely, recall a moment when you respected your partner's perspective. How can you both continue to foster respect within your relationship?

MY NOTES

Finding Compromise: Reflect on a disagreement you and your partner resolved through compromise. Describe the process of finding common ground, and how it strengthened your relationship.

MY NOTES

What strategies can help you both navigate future disagreements more effectively?

MY NOTES

Quality Time Together: List five activities you enjoy doing with your partner and five new activities you'd like to try together.

MY NOTES

How can you prioritize quality time in your busy schedules?

MY NOTES

Support System: Recall a time when your partner supported you during a challenging situation or encouraged you to pursue a goal. How did their support impact you?

MY NOTES

Write about a moment when you offered support to your partner and its outcome.

MY NOTES

Physical Affection: Reflect on the role physical affection plays in your relationship. Are you both comfortable with the level of physical touch?

MY NOTES

Share some examples of how you express physical affection, and discuss any changes you'd like to see.

MY NOTES

Gratitude and Appreciation: Write down three things you're grateful for in your relationship and three qualities you appreciate about your partner.

MY NOTES

MY NOTES

LOVE

"twuu wuv" - Princess Bride

A chapter on love could turn into a series of books on this one topic alone; I'm just going to give you the cliff notes version.

Love can change and evolve throughout a relationship, whether it be a romantic relationship or a friendship. Love is an essential component in any relationship, whether it be a romantic relationship or a friendship.

Here are some reasons why love is needed in a relationship:

Connection: Love allows us to form meaningful connections with others, promoting a sense of belonging and fulfillment.

Emotional Support: Love provides emotional support during difficult times, helping us feel valued and understood by the people around us.

Growth: Love motivates us to improve ourselves and strive for personal growth, as we want to be the best version of ourselves for the people we care about.

Trust: Love fosters a sense of confidence and security in a relationship, allowing us to be vulnerable with our partners and friends.

Happiness: Love brings joy and happiness into our lives, creating meaningful and fulfilling experiences.

It's important to note that love is not a cure-all for all problems in a relationship. It takes effort, commitment, and communication to maintain a strong and healthy connection with others. However, love can be a powerful catalyst in building and maintaining healthy, enriching relationships in our lives.

In a romantic relationship, love tends to start off as an intense feeling of infatuation. As the relationship progresses, this feeling may develop into a deep and profound attachment to the other person. This attachment becomes a solid foundation for a long-term committed relationship. Over time, as the relationship deepens, love can take on different forms, such as a deep sense of companionship, a commitment to working through challenges and growing together, and a sense of comfort and security.

In a friendship, love can also evolve in different ways. Initially, love in a friendship may grow from a shared interest or experience. As friendships deepen, love can take on a sense of loyalty, trust, and respect for the other person. In some cases, the love in a friendship can be likened to that of a sibling, with people becoming like chosen family members. For many people, "family" refers to more than just blood relatives; it includes close friends and other individuals who have become like family.

These individuals are often referred to as "chosen family," and recognizing the role they play in our lives is vital for many reasons, such as providing emotional support. Chosen family members are the ones in your life that are there to provide emotional support during challenging times, offering a listening ear and a shoulder to lean on when you need it. A family does not mean only being related by blood; a family embodies so much more than just DNA. Chosen family members unconditionally love and accept us for who we are without judgment or expectation. Selected family members foster a sense of belonging and community, providing a network of people who share similar values and beliefs. Chosen family members often share experiences and milestones that create deep bonds and lasting memories. Selected family members can help build resilience in our lives, providing a source of strength and support during times of adversity.

Recognizing the critical role of chosen family members

can help us prioritize these relationships in our lives and cultivate strong and meaningful connections with those we love. It's important to remember that we have the power to create and shape our families in ways that reflect our values, beliefs, and needs.

It's important to note that the ever-evolving nature of love doesn't necessarily mean that the intensity of the feeling diminishes over time. Instead, love may grow and deepen in many ways, taking on different forms as the relationship evolves. As we continue to grow and change throughout our lives, love has the potential to do the same, bringing new and exciting elements to our relationships, both romantic and friendly.

MANY DIFFERENT TYPES OF LOVE

- Romantic Love is the love typically associated with a committed relationship between two physically and emotionally attracted individuals.

- Platonic Love refers to a deep friendship between two people and does not involve a romantic or physical relationship.

- Familial Love is the love between family members, such as parents and children, siblings, and extended family members / chosen family members.

- Self-Love - This refers to the practice of caring for and prioritizing one's personal needs and learning to love oneself fully and unconditionally.

- Unrequited Love - This is a type of love where one person has strong feelings for another, but those feelings are not reciprocated.

- Agape Love - This is selfless, unconditional love that seeks to serve others and put their needs before one's own. Agape was later translated into Latin as caritas, which is the origin of our word "charity."

☐ Obsessive Love - This is a type of love that can become unhealthy and borders on stalking behavior, where one person fixates on another to an unhealthy degree.

Understanding different types of love can be beneficial in several ways. First, it can help us recognize how love can be expressed and experienced, allowing us to appreciate and respect the diversity of human relationships. Additionally, understanding different types of love can help us navigate and maintain healthy relationships as we become more aware of our own needs and the needs of those around us. It can also help us recognize when a relationship is unhealthy or unbalanced and give us tools to work towards a more equitable and fulfilling love connection. Understanding different types of love, we can deepen our own ability to love and be loved, bringing more joy, connection, and fulfillment into our lives.

Genuine connections can provide comfort and understanding, helping us build emotional resilience and cope with challenges more effectively. We also discover different perspectives, develop new skills, and gain valuable insights into the world — all through sharing experiences with people we care about. Having meaningful connections with people allows us to explore different perspectives, develop new skills, and gain valuable insights into the world. So don't forget to take the time to invest in your relationships — it's vital to personal development.

It's not just our minds that benefit from having relationships — our bodies do, too! Studies show that people with strong social networks have lower risks of heart disease, strokes, and even some types of cancer. Plus, they get sick less often and recover faster. So not only are relationships good for our mental health, but they can also help keep us physically healthy. There are so many studies out there supporting this; just google it, and you will see pages and pages of research supporting the idea that healthy relationships have physical benefits to our health, such as a person having fewer stress hormones and even healing quicker. Even studies show that it can help you live longer; I love science!

Humans are social creatures — we need relationships to survive and thrive. Connecting with others is essential for our emotional, mental, and physical well-being. It helps boost our self-esteem, reduce stress levels, improve communication skills, and even increase overall life satisfaction. But remember, no relationship is perfect. There will be times when it gets tough, and you'll have to work at it. It might involve communicating more openly, compromising on some issues, or simply finding new ways to show appreciation and love. Having meaningful connections requires active effort, but by putting in the work, you'll get stronger bonds. All of these things take effort, but in the end, it's worth it for a stronger, healthier relationship!

WHY CAN'T I MAKE SOMEONE LOVE ME?

It is not possible to make someone love you; feelings of love cannot be forced, coerced, or manipulated. Love involves the mutual feeling of care and respect that two people have for each other. It is something that must develop organically between two individuals, often over some time. The best way to increase your chances of being loved is to be open and honest with the other person, show them respect and kindness, and support their choices.

While it may be true that being able to change is an important part of growing up and becoming a responsible adult. While trying to force someone to change may be tempting, this can often lead to unintended consequences. We cannot make somebody else change; at best, we can help inspire them toward positive action.

For example, if a person's behavior is causing a strain in their relationship, it's better to talk about the issue openly and honestly. Offer understanding and compassion towards them first, then provide them with resources that may help them make changes if they choose to do so. Let them know you're there for support should they need it. Doing this shows respect for their autonomy and allows them to take ownership of their choices.

It's important to remember that change doesn't happen overnight. It takes time, dedication, and commitment for real transformation to occur. Rather than forcing someone to conform to our expectations, we should support them through the process with patience and understanding. Ultimately, helping someone change is not about us; it's about the person we're trying to help.

Whatever our intentions may be, boundary violations will only impede their progress rather than aid it—and that's something we should all strive to avoid. So when your friend or loved one needs guidance, provide them with the resources they need and remind them you're there to support them. This is the best way to help someone make meaningful, lasting changes in their lives.

Regarding helping those around us, respect and understanding are vital components of successful boundary-setting. We must remember our responsibility is not to control another person's choices or dictate how they should live their lives. Instead, we can provide them with the tools and resources to help guide them in the direction they need to go.

The thought, "why can't they love me'; is unhealthy because it puts pressure on the other person to conform to our expectations and can create an imbalance in the relationship. It can also lead to feelings of resentment and sabotage a person's sense of autonomy. When we attempt to control someone else's choices, we are imposing our own will upon them, which can be damaging to both parties. Instead of trying to control or manipulate someone, we should give them the freedom and respect to make their own choices. This will help create an atmosphere of trust and understanding in the relationship, which is ultimately healthier for everyone involved.

When someone tries to win someone else's love, it could indicate their lack of self-esteem and self-love. They may feel incomplete without someone else's affection and validation. Such feelings usually stem from insecurity and low self-worth.

1. Think about a time when you tried to make someone love you. How did that affect your feelings of self-worth? Write about what you learned from that experience.

MY NOTES

MY NOTES

2.Describe a moment when you realized that you can't make someone love you. How did this realization change the way you see yourself and your relationships?

MY NOTES

MY NOTES

3. Write about ways you can show love and appreciation for yourself, even when others may not reciprocate your feelings. How can practicing self-love improve your self-worth?

MY NOTES

MY NOTES

4. Reflect on the importance of respecting other people's feelings and choices, even if it means they don't love you back. How can accepting this truth help you grow as a person?

MY NOTES

MY NOTES

5. List three positive qualities you have that make you worthy of love. Write about how you can remind yourself of these qualities when you feel down or unloved.

MY NOTES

MY NOTES

4 Quick Ways to See if Your Relationship is Thriving

Sometimes it can be hard to tell if your relationships are going well or not. Luckily, there are a few tell-tale signs that you can look out for to make sure everything is on the right track.

Here are some things to watch for:

1. Spending time together - If you and your partner make time to hang out regularly, then it's a good sign that things are going well.

2. Mutual Respect - Respect is one of the critical components of any healthy relationship. If you both treat each other with respect, then it shows that both parties value the other person's opinion and feelings.

3. Open communication - Talking about how you feel and listening to each other's perspectives is an essential part of a strong relationship. If you can communicate openly, then it's likely that things will go well.

4. Having fun - Relationships should be enjoyable for both parties! If you're laughing together and having a good time, then it's a sign that your relationship is strong and healthy.

These are just a few signs that your relationships are going well. Paying attention to these indicators can give you an idea of how things are going, so remember to keep an eye out for them!

STAGES OF A ROMANTIC RELATIONSHIP

The different stages of a romantic relationship can vary depending on the source, with some models suggesting four stages while others suggest six or more. However, the general stages are commonly understood to be:

1. Infatuation or attraction stage
2. The romantic stage
3. The stability stage
4. The commitment stage
5. The co-creation or partnership stage
6. The blissful love stage

Knowing about these stages can help us understand and navigate our own relationships. It can also provide a framework for evaluating where we are in a relationship and what we might need to work on to progress to the next stage. For example, if a couple is stuck in the romantic stage and struggling to move into the stability stage, they may need to work on communication and conflict resolution skills.

By knowing what stage our relationship is in, we can tailor our communication style to suit our needs. For example, in the stability stage, we may need to focus on maintaining a sense of connection and intimacy, while in the commitment stage, we may need to have more discussions around shared goals and the future.

Understanding these stages can also help us manage our expectations and avoid common pitfalls. For example, in the infatuation or attraction stage, we may idealize our partner and overlook potential red flags. By recognizing this stage for what it is, we can make more informed decisions about whether to pursue a deeper relationship.

Having a clear understanding of the different stages can also prevent unnecessary anxiety and stress. If our relationship seems to be stuck in one stage or isn't progressing as quickly as we had hoped, we may feel worried or discouraged. However, knowing that each stage takes time and effort to evolve can provide reassurance and help us stay patient and committed.

Ultimately, while the number of stages can vary, the importance of understanding the general trajectory of a romantic relationship remains the same. It can help us build stronger, healthier relationships and achieve a deeper sense of intimacy and connection with our partners.

Examples of Each Stage:

Infatuation or attraction stage: In this stage, couples feel a strong attraction to each other and may spend a lot of time together. They might constantly text or call each other, and find it hard to focus on anything else. It's exciting and fun, but it's important to remember that this stage doesn't last forever. Be mindful of not losing sight of your individual interests and friendships.

The romantic stage: Couples in this stage are deeply in love and enjoy spending time together. They often go on dates, share special moments, and may start saying "I love you." While it's great to feel so connected, be careful not to idealize your partner too much, as this can lead to disappointment when they don't meet unrealistic expectations.

The stability stage: As the relationship matures, couples begin to feel more comfortable and secure with each other. They might move in together or start making long-term plans. This stage can bring a sense of calm, but it's crucial to maintain open communication and work through any issues that arise to avoid becoming complacent.

The commitment stage: In this stage, couples decide to make a lasting commitment to each other, such as getting engaged or married. They have a solid foundation and trust in their relationship. However, it's essential to continue nurturing the relationship, as taking each other for granted can lead to problems down the line.

The co-creation or partnership stage: Here, couples may start building a life together, like having children or starting a business. They work as a team and support each other's goals. While it's rewarding to create something together, it's important to balance personal needs with shared responsibilities and maintain a strong emotional connection.

The blissful love stage: In this stage, couples have a deep understanding of each other and a strong bond. They appreciate their partner's quirks and have a sense of contentment. While this stage is beautiful, it's still essential to keep the spark alive by regularly expressing love and appreciation and continuing to grow together.

By understanding these stages and being mindful of potential challenges, couples can navigate their relationship journey in a supportive and fulfilling way, regardless of their unique circumstances.

1. What values are important to me when it comes to my relationship with myself?

MY NOTES

2. How do I show respect for myself?

MY NOTES

3. What boundaries have I set for myself and why?

MY NOTES

4. What expectations have I established for myself when it comes to my emotional wellbeing and self-care?

MY NOTES

5. How can I cultivate more meaningful relationships with myself and others?

MY NOTES

6 What do I need to feel supported in my relationships?

MY NOTES

7. How can I be a better listener, communicator and respecter of boundaries for myself and those around me?

MY NOTES

8. What steps can I take to ensure that my relationships are healthy and fulfilling?

MY NOTES

These reflective journal questions can help you gain insight into yourself, your values, your needs, and the boundaries and expectations you have established for yourself. Answering them honestly can help you create positive and supportive relationships with both you and those around you. By understanding what is important to you in a relationship, taking responsibility for your well-being, communicating openly, and respecting boundaries, you can create meaningful relationships that are positive and supportive. Taking the time to practice these tips and skills will help ensure your relationships are successful and fulfilling.

BOUNDARIES

One cannot have a healthy relationship without a healthy boundary. A healthy boundary in a relationship is the respect of each person's limits and individual autonomy. Boundaries allow us to remain emotionally and physically safe, set clear expectations for our relationships, and maintain relationships with ourselves and others. It is important to remember that boundaries can be different for every relationship – what might work for one may not work for another. Good boundaries can help build trust and keep each person's needs in mind, so it is essential to talk about your expectations with the other person. Establishing healthy boundaries also includes recognizing when a boundary has been crossed, speaking up if needed, and respecting each other's limits.

Boundaries are like a "rulebook" that helps us stay safe and get along with other people. They help us figure out what is okay and not okay in relationships so we know how to act with each other. Having boundaries also helps us make sure all our needs are met. They might include things like respecting each other's space or taking turns talking when we disagree on something. It is essential to talk about your boundaries with the people you care about so that everyone can be happy and feel safe.

Boundaries have always been an essential part of relationships, but in recent years they have become much more popular. This can be attributed to the increased focus on mental health, as well as the development of new communication and relationship skills. Boundaries help us create healthy connections with other people by letting us express our needs and expectations clearly and setting limits on how we interact with each other. This helps us stay safe and be respected while also cultivating a feeling of trust and security in relationships. By understanding boundaries, we can better maintain our own well-being and that of others, leading to deeper connections and happier lives.

I like to describe a boundary as a friendly reminder to help us get along better with other people, while an ultimatum is more like a demand. With a boundary, we might politely ask someone to respect our space or give us time to think before making decisions. On the other hand, an ultimatum often involves threats or demands – for example, "Do what I say or else!"

Boundaries help us build better relationships because they

show respect and consideration. Ultimatums can be ineffective and even damaging to relationships because they make the other person feel inferior and powerless. In short, boundaries are friendly requests that help us stay safe and respect each other's needs, while ultimatums involve making threats or demands.

Here are some examples :

Example 1:

Boundary "I would really appreciate it if you could give me a few minutes to cool off before we talk about this issue."

Ultimatum: "If you don't do what I'm asking, then I'm not going to talk to you ever again!"

"Get away from me now!"

Example 2:

Boundary: "Please respect my space and give me time to think before making decisions in our relationship."

Ultimatum: "If you don't do what I say, then our relationship is over!"

Example 3:

Boundary: "I need some time alone to process things before we have a conversation about them."

Ultimatum: "If you don't do what I say, I won't talk to you ever again!"

"Just shut up!"

Example 4:

Boundary: "Please respect my decision and don't try to change my mind about this matter."

Ultimatum: "Either you do what I say, or there will be serious consequences!"

Boundaries are like a way of setting expectations in relationships so that everyone can be happy and feel safe. Examples of boundaries might include things like respecting each other's space, taking turns talking when there's an argument, or agreeing to communicate honestly with each other.

Ultimatums, on the other hand, involve demands or threats. It is not a healthy way to communicate and can often lead to more tension in relationships. Examples of ultimatums could include things like demanding someone change their behavior or threatening to end the relationship if they don't do what you want them to do. Ultimately, boundaries are beneficial for cultivating respectful, trusting relationships, whereas ultimatums can be harmful and damaging.

WHAT IS THE IMPORTANCE OF ENFORCING BOUNDARIES?

Enforcing boundaries is essential for any healthy relationship, as it helps us feel safe and respected by others. By setting firm boundaries and following through with them, we can communicate our needs and expectations to others in a clear and respectful way. This can help us form strong relationships based on mutual trust and understanding. Additionally, boundaries allow us to establish personal limits so that we don't feel taken advantage of or disrespected by others.

Enforcing a boundary in a respectful way can be difficult, as it requires us to communicate our needs and expectations to others in a clear and direct manner. To do this effectively, we must remain calm and stay firm in our stance while also being understanding of the other person's perspective.

Using "I" statements to express our feelings, rather than blaming the other person by using "you" is so very important- if you get nothing out of this book other than that – you will be all the happier because of it. It is also essential to remain consistent with our boundaries, as this will demonstrate that we respect ourselves and are standing up for our own needs.

Ultimately, while it can be difficult to enforce a boundary in a respectful way at times, it is essential for maintaining healthy relationships. I realize that using "I" statements might sound simple to you, but honestly, it is magic! When you use "you," it's as if the person is putting earplugs in and the conversation is done, but when you use "I,", especially with a feeling word, it's as if a light bulb went on and the person understands you – try it! Totally magic- sometimes, it's the simple solutions in life that have the most significant impact.

Example of "I" vs. "You" Statements

Examples of "I" statements that can be used when establishing boundaries include:
-"I would really appreciate it if you could give me some space right now."
-"I don't feel comfortable with lying, so I need to be honest when talking to you."
-"I'm not okay with being treated this way, and I need you to respect my boundaries."
-"I'm feeling overwhelmed and need some time for myself."

On the other hand, "you" statements can come across as accusatory or aggressive and should be avoided when establishing boundaries.

Examples of "you" statements include:

-"You always make me feel bad when you talk to me like that."

-"You need to stop lying to me."

-"You're making me feel uncomfortable with your behavior."

-"You should respect my boundaries and give me some space."

By using "I" statements when establishing boundaries, we can communicate our thoughts and feelings in a respectful manner.

WHY

Boundaries help us build better relationships because they show respect and consideration. Ultimatums can be ineffective and even damaging to relationships because they make the other person feel inferior and powerless. It's important to talk about boundaries because it helps us create a safe and healthy environment for everyone involved. When we establish boundaries with the people we care about, we can make sure that our needs are met and respected while also respecting theirs. Talking openly and honestly about our boundaries helps us all better understand each other and find common ground.

Overall, setting boundaries is an essential step in fostering meaningful relationships. It helps us feel respected and secure while still allowing us to be open and honest with others. By understanding the difference between boundaries and ultimatums, we can make sure that everyone's needs are met while staying true to ourselves.

Creating healthy boundaries is an essential step toward building meaningful relationships. Knowing what you want from a relationship and setting expectations will help others understand your needs. When expressing your boundaries, be clear with yourself and the people you interact with about what those boundaries are and any consequences for breaking them. Being open and honest can foster mutual respect and understanding between all parties involved.

Expressing your "why" or reason for setting a boundary is essential in communicating effectively with others. When you express your "why" in a boundary, it helps clarify the reasoning behind it, making it easier for others to understand where you're coming from. Expressing your "why" can help legitimize your boundary. This helps establish the severity of the boundary and why it's essential to follow it. You are respecting the other person by giving them a clear understanding of why you've set the boundary. This can help promote a more positive and respectful relationship between you and the other person.

To figure out your "why," here are 4 practical steps that can help:

1. Reflect: Take time to reflect on your values, goals, and personal needs. Consider what is important to you and what makes you happy.

2. Identify: Identify situations or behaviors that make you feel

uncomfortable, anxious, or upset. These can point to areas where boundaries need to be set.

3. Prioritize: Prioritize what boundaries are most important to you and why. Consider the consequences of not setting those boundaries and how they may impact your well-being.

4. Communicate: Once you've established your "why," communicate it effectively with others. Start by stating the boundary, followed by the reason why it's important to you.

By expressing your "why" in a boundary, you are helping communicate with others in a way that is effective, respectful, and promotes trust. It also helps establish clear guidelines and promotes a healthier relationship.

Establishing boundaries can help you feel more in control of your relationships while also reducing stress and anxiety. Healthy boundaries will ensure that everyone is feeling respected and supported! Setting boundaries is different from issuing ultimatums - instead of demanding something or threatening a consequence, focus on creating an open dialogue about expectations. When having this discussion, be sure to remain respectful and open-minded so that all parties involved can come to an agreement on what is acceptable. Doing this will ensure that everyone's needs are being respected while still fostering meaningful relationships.

Healthy vs Unhealthy Boundaries

Healthy:
* people know where they stand
* give room for discussion allow all parties to be on the same page guidelines, rules, limits, or expectations
* are created to identify reasonable, safe, and permissible ways for other people to treat you.
*your response or the consequences you'll carry out if and when those limits are overstepped or violated.

Boundaries create a safe space for you.

Unhealthy
*You make them for only 1 person.
*You make them around a person's behavior that you want to control.
*You are not consistent

CONNECTION

My wife's love language is a physical connection like cuddling and hugs, but I don't like to cuddle so this at times can cause some friction. I can't sleep if I can't move it just does not work for me. Mine, I guess, would be acts or actions or something like that - Confession I've never read the book, just articles about it. I love anything that gets couples working on their relationship and figuring out ways to connect with one another. I am not a fan of how some individuals use the book on love languages to either keep score or as a quick fix. Love languages are fluid and can change and adapt over time.

Connection is significant in any relationship, platonic or not, and understanding how others like to receive affection and connection is also essential. Learning this about yourself and those you interact with is excellent. My word of caution is that just because you know someone's love language does not mean it is the only way that love should be shown to that person.

Love languages can be a great tool to help couples figure

out how to best connect with each other and create meaningful relationships! But it's essential to take the time to really get to know your partner so you understand how they like to receive affection and connection. It's also important to remember that just because you know someone's love language doesn't mean you have to be comfortable with it, or it is the only way to show them love. It's an excellent opportunity for couples to talk about how they want to make connections, what that looks like, how it works within their boundaries, and to consider compromises. Ultimately, by investing in yourself, communicating openly, understanding your values and needs, showing respect, and knowing when it's time to take a step back, you can make sure that your relationships are healthy and fulfilling.

1. How does understanding someone's love language help create meaningful relationships?

MY NOTES

2. What are some tips for communicating openly and respecting boundaries in a relationship?

MY NOTES

MY NOTES

3. Why is it important to take the time to get to know your partner?

MY NOTES

MY NOTES

4. How can couples make sure their relationships are healthy and fulfilling?

MY NOTES

5. What compromises might be necessary to ensure a successful relationship?

MY NOTES

6. How do our own values and needs impact the relationships we have with others?

MY NOTES

7. How can taking responsibility for your own wellbeing help create positive relationships?

MY NOTES

Worksheet 1:
Understanding the Difference between Boundaries and Ultimatums

1 What are boundaries?
_____
_____
_____

2 What is one boundary that you would like to establish in your relationships?
_____
_____
_____

3 Write an example or two of "I" statements that you are going to use in a future conversation:
_____
_____
_____

4 What are ultimatums?
_____
_____
_____

5 What are the benefits of understanding the difference between boundaries & ultimatums?
_____
_____
_____

6 What areas can you improve upon?
_____
_____
_____

Answer Key

Worksheet 1:
Understanding the Difference between Boundaries and Ultimatums

1. Boundaries are firm but friendly requests that respect everyone's needs. They help us to foster healthy and respectful relationships, by communicating our thoughts and feelings in a respectful manner.

2. could be around time, feelings, topics, physical

3. Examples of "I" statements used when establishing boundaries include: "I would really appreciate it if you could give me some space right now," or "I don't feel comfortable with lying, so I need to be honest when talking to you."

4. Ultimatums are more like threats or demands. They involve making threats or demands in order to get what we want and can be ineffective or even damaging to relationships. Examples of "you" statements used when issuing ultimatums include: "You always make me feel bad when you talk to me like that," or "You should respect my boundaries and give me some space."

5. Understanding the difference between boundaries and ultimatums helps us create a safe and healthy environment for everyone involved. It allows us to make sure our needs met and respected while still respecting people's needs. It also us build better relationships by showing respect and consideration.

6. be honest with yourself - what areas in communication and/or setting up healthy boundaries could you use some practice in?

Worksheet 2: How to Set Boundaries and Respect Others' Needs

1 Identify what your own boundaries are:

___

2 Rewrite them in "I" statements; clearly and respectfully:

___

3 What boundaries have you been asked to respect in your current relationships?

___

4 Are there any boundaries that need to be discussed and agreed upon? If so what are they and how can you come to a compromise?

___

5 How can you make sure that you are following someone's boundary?

___

6 What areas can you improve upon?

___

Answer Key

Worksheet 2: How to Set Boundaries and Respect Others' Needs

1. Start by reflecting on what your needs and boundaries are, such as respecting someone's physical or emotional space, being honest about your feelings, or other specific requests.

2. Communicate them clearly and respectfully: Once you have identified what your boundaries are, communicate them to the other person in a respectful and clear manner. Use "I" statements to express how you feel without pointing fingers or making accusations. For example, instead of saying "You always make me feel uncomfortable when you do that," say "I don't like it when you do that, and I need more space."

3. Respect other people's boundaries: Just as we expect others to respect our boundaries, it is important to respect their boundaries too. Ask for permission before doing something that may violate someone else's boundaries. Listen to and validate their feelings.

4. Be open to negotiation and compromise: Negotiation and compromise is often necessary when setting boundaries with others. When both parties understand what each needs, it can be easier to find a solution that works for everyone.

5. Check-in regularly: Establishing boundaries is an ongoing process. Check-in regularly with yourself and others to make sure boundaries are still being respected and adjust them if needed.

6. be honest with yourself - what areas in communication and/or setting up healthy boundaries could you use some practice in?

RELATIONSHIPS WITH KIDDOS

If you're under the impression that this chapter doesn't concern you because you don't have kids, think again. Every single one of us was once a child, and it's crucial to explore your own experiences with your parent(s) during that time. Trust me, understanding and reflecting on these relationships can significantly impact your present and future relationships. So, take a deep breath and dive into this chapter with an open mind. You won't regret it.

The bond between a parent and their child plays a crucial role in the child's growth and development. When a child receives love, support, and understanding from their parent, it positively influences their overall development. A loving and stable relationship with your child helps them to become effective thinkers. By providing a safe and secure environment, you create a space for your child to explore and learn about the world around them. This allows them to develop critical thinking skills and become better problem solvers as they grow older.

Responsive parenting helps children to understand how to deal with their emotions. When parents acknowledge and validate their child's feelings, it helps children to develop greater emotional intelligence and awareness. This, in turn, helps children learn how to manage their emotions in a healthy way, which can have a positive impact on their relationships later in life.

A supportive relationship with your child can help them develop strong social skills. By modeling positive behaviors and demonstrating empathy and understanding, you are teaching your child how to interact with others in a healthy and respectful way. This can help them form strong friendships and relationships throughout their life.

Ultimately, the relationship between parent and child has a significant impact on a child's long-term development. Children who experience a loving and stable relationship with their parents are more likely to develop into well-adjusted, emotionally intelligent adults who are capable of building strong relationships with others.

PARENTING STYLES & THEIR IMPACT

When it comes to parenting, there are four main styles that experts in child psychology recognize: permissive, authoritative, neglectful, and authoritarian. Diana Baumrind, a developmental psychologist, first identified these styles and was later expanded upon by Stanford researchers Eleanor Maccoby and John Martin.

Let's take a closer look at each style:

Permissive parents tend to be very laid-back and lenient, often letting their children do whatever they want without setting many rules or boundaries. While this may seem carefree, it can lead to children feeling insecure and unsure of what's expected of them. As an adult whom permissive parents raised, you may struggle with setting and maintaining boundaries in your own relationships and may have difficulty making decisions.

Examples of permissive parenting:

- Allowing a child to make their own rules and decisions without any guidance or structure

- Failing to set boundaries or enforce consequences for negative behavior

- Giving in to a child's every demand or request, even if it is not in their best interest or goes against family rules

- Avoiding discipline or punishment altogether, in fear of upsetting the child or damaging the relationship

- Tolerating disrespectful or rude behavior from a child without addressing it

- Ignoring or minimizing serious issues such as substance abuse, mental health problems, or criminal behavior.

Authoritative parents, on the other hand, are warm and loving but also set clear expectations and boundaries for their children. They value open communication and encourage their children to express their thoughts and feelings. This style tends to produce confident, independent children who are able to make good decisions. As an adult whom authoritative parents raised, you likely have strong communication skills and are able to assert yourself in work and personal relationships.

Examples of authoritative parenting:

- Setting clear and consistent rules and expectations for behavior
- Using positive reinforcement and praise to encourage good behavior and discourage negative behavior
- Providing reasoning and explanations for rules and decisions, while also being open to feedback and discussion
- Enforcing consequences for negative behavior that are fair and consistent with the severity of the behavior
- Encouraging independence and decision-making skills while also providing guidance and support
- Taking an interest in a child's life and activities, and supporting their interests and aspirations
- Teaching important values such as respect, empathy, responsibility, and self-control.

Neglectful parents are often emotionally distant and uninvolved in their children's lives. They may not set any rules or boundaries at all and may not offer emotional support or guidance. This can lead to children feeling neglected and insecure, which can have long-lasting impacts on their mental health and relationships. As an adult whom neglectful parents raised, you may struggle with self-esteem and may have difficulty forming solid relationships.

Examples of neglectful parenting:
- Failing to provide basic physical needs such as food, clothing, and shelter
- Ignoring a child's emotional needs such as comfort, love, and support
- Failing to provide necessary medical care or education
- Leaving a child unattended for long periods of time, or frequently leaving them in the care of others without proper supervision
- Showing little interest or involvement in a child's life and activities
- Failing to set any rules, boundaries, or guidelines for behavior
- Refusing to acknowledge or address concerning behavior or issues within the family

Authoritarian parents are strict and controlling, often using punishment as a way to keep their children in line. While this may result in well-behaved children, it can also stifle creativity and lead to resentment and rebellion. As an adult whom authoritarian parents raised, you may struggle with feeling like you need to be in control all the time and may have difficulty trusting others.

Examples of authoritarian parenting:
- Setting strict and rigid rules without explanation or flexibility
- Using punishment and negative reinforcement to control behavior
- Showing little warmth or affection towards the child
- Discouraging independence and decision-making skills
- Focusing on obedience and respect for authority above all else
- Using fear tactics or intimidation to gain compliance
- Failing to acknowledge or address a child's emotional needs, such as comfort, love, and support.

It's important to note that no parenting style is perfect, and each has its own strengths and weaknesses. However, by understanding how your own parents' style impacted you, you can work to overcome any negative impacts and foster healthy relationships as an adult.

ATTACHMENT

Attachment relationships are incredibly important for a child's development, and research has found that there are at least four different attachment categories that children can fall into. These categories help to describe the ways that children act and interact with both their parents and caregivers.

The strongest kind of attachment is called "secure." Children who have a secure attachment with their caregivers feel safe, loved, and supported. They are able to explore their environment with confidence, knowing that their caregiver is nearby if they need them. As adults, those who had a secure attachment with their caregivers are more likely to have healthy relationships with others.

Examples of secure attachment styles in adults:
- Feeling comfortable with emotional intimacy and closeness in relationships
- Able to communicate openly and honestly about feelings and needs

- Trusting and supportive of romantic partners and close friends
- Showing empathy and understanding towards the emotions and needs of others
- Able to maintain healthy boundaries in relationships without feeling threatened or anxious
- Having a positive self-image and sense of self-worth
- Able to effectively resolve conflicts and misunderstandings in relationships.

Another type of attachment is called "avoidant." Children with an avoidant attachment tend to avoid their caregivers, and may seem indifferent to their presence. They may not seek comfort when they are upset, and may appear to be emotionally distant. As adults, those who had an avoidant attachment may struggle with intimacy and have difficulty forming close relationships.

Examples of avoidant attachment in adults:
- Struggling with intimacy and avoiding close relationships
- Feeling uncomfortable or anxious when someone becomes too emotionally close or dependent
- Downplaying or dismissing the importance of emotional connection in relationships

- Feeling uncomfortable sharing personal information or feelings with others
- Being self-reliant to the point of avoiding seeking help or support from others
- Showing a lack of interest or concern for the emotional needs of others
- Preferring to keep relationships superficial or at a distance to avoid vulnerability or emotional risk.

A third type of attachment is called "ambivalent." Children with an ambivalent attachment may seem to cling to their caregivers, but may also be angry or resistant when their caregiver returns after a separation. As adults, those with an ambivalent attachment may struggle with insecurity in their relationships and may have difficulty trusting others.

Examples of ambivalent attachment in adults:
- Constantly seeking reassurance and validation from romantic partners or close friends
- Experiencing anxiety or distress when separated from loved ones, even for short periods of time
- Feeling a strong need for emotional closeness but also fearing abandonment or rejection
- Difficulty trusting others and often questioning their

motives or intentions

- Tendency to become overly dependent on others for emotional support
- Struggling with self-esteem and self-worth, often feeling unworthy of love or care
- Inconsistent behavior in relationships, alternating between being clingy and pushing others away.

Finally, some children have a "disorganized" attachment, which can be caused by inconsistent or abusive caregiving. These children may seem confused or disoriented and may show unusual behavior, such as freezing or rocking. As adults, those with disorganized attachment may struggle with emotional regulation and may experience difficulties in relationships.

Examples of an adult who was raised with a disorganized parenting style:

- Difficulty forming and maintaining stable relationships due to conflicting desires for closeness and distance
- Struggling with trust issues and often feeling suspicious or fearful of others' intentions
- Exhibiting erratic and unpredictable behavior in relationships, causing confusion for themselves and their partners

- Experiencing intense emotional reactions, such as sudden anger or sadness, without a clear understanding of the cause
- Struggling with self-esteem, self-worth, and self-identity, leading to feelings of insecurity and instability
- Difficulty setting and maintaining healthy boundaries in relationships, resulting in codependency or manipulation
- Having trouble regulating emotions and coping with stress, often leading to impulsive decisions or self-destructive behaviors.

If you are concerned about your child's attachment style, there are steps you can take to help improve your relationship with them. One way is to make sure you respond to your child's needs consistently, so they feel safe and supported. You can also try to be more attuned to your child's emotions and help them develop their emotional intelligence. Finally, seeking professional help from a therapist or counselor can be beneficial if you struggle to form a healthy attachment with your child.

I'M ALREADY AN ADULT; IS IT TOO LATE FOR ME?

As an adult, it's possible to work on changing your attachment style in order to develop healthier relationships in the future. Here are some specific steps you can take:

Practice self-awareness: Start by becoming aware of your own attachment style and how it impacts your relationships. This may involve reflecting on your past experiences and recognizing patterns that have emerged in your relationships.

Seek therapy: Working with a therapist can be incredibly helpful in addressing attachment issues. A therapist can help you identify underlying issues that may be contributing to your attachment style and teach you new skills to improve your relationships.

Learn to communicate effectively: Communication is key in any relationship, and it's especially important for those with attachment issues. Practice being open and honest with your partner, and try to be more attuned to their emotions as well.

Build trust: If you struggle with trust issues, make an effort to build trust in your relationships. This may involve setting small goals and following through on them, or simply being reliable and consistent in your actions.

Work on emotional regulation: If you tend to be overly emotional or reactive, it's important to work on regulating your emotions. This might involve practicing mindfulness or other relaxation techniques, or seeking out additional support from a mental health professional.

Remember that changing your attachment style is a process, and it may take time and effort to see progress. But with patience and perseverance, it's possible to develop healthier, more fulfilling relationships in the future.

SO IT'S ALL MY PARENT'S FAULT

Blaming your parents for everything that's wrong in your life can be tempting, especially if you had a difficult or traumatic childhood. However, while it may feel cathartic at the moment, blaming your parents is not an effective way to heal or change. Now don't get me wrong we as parents we all mess up; I just as a therapist I have greater insight into how much I "f... ed up " and I have a list of future therapists my kids can see when they are older.

One reason why blaming your parents isn't helpful is that it can keep you stuck in the past. By focusing on what your parents did wrong, you're not able to move forward and make positive changes in your life. This can lead to feelings of anger, resentment, and helplessness, which can further inhibit your ability to grow and develop as a person. You have every right to be upset with them and have mixed emotions I'm just cautioning about staying in that state of mind.

Another reason why blaming your parents is ineffective is that it's often not entirely accurate. While it's true that our childhood experiences can have a significant impact on our development, it's important to recognize that we are ultimately responsible for our own lives as adults. We have the power to make choices and take action to create the life we want, even if our upbringing was less than perfect. If they were monsters; that sucks and you have the right to feel cheated and grieve the parents you never got, but you also are an adult now reading this book so it's time to take action and help yourself heal.

Finally, blaming your parents can prevent you from developing healthy relationships with others. If you're constantly focused on what your parents did wrong, you may struggle to trust others or form close connections. This can lead to feelings of loneliness and isolation, which can have negative impacts on your mental health and overall well-being.

Instead of blaming your parents, try to focus on what you can do to heal and grow as a person. This may involve seeking therapy, practicing self-care, and working on developing healthy habits and relationships. Remember that while your past experiences may have shaped who you are today, they don't have to determine your future. You have the power to create the life you want, regardless of what happened in the past.

1. Which parenting style(s) do you believe your parents or caregivers used while raising you? How did this shape your childhood experiences?

MY NOTES

2. How has the parenting style you experienced influenced your own approach to relationships, communication, and trust in adulthood?

MY NOTES

3. Are there any specific examples from your childhood that stand out as particularly positive or negative in terms of how your parents or caregivers interacted with you?

MY NOTES

4. In what ways do you think your upbringing has contributed to your strengths and weaknesses as an adult?

MY NOTES

5. If you could change one aspect of the parenting style you experienced, what would it be and why?

MY NOTES

6. How has your understanding of different parenting styles influenced your thoughts on how you might parent (or currently parent) your own children?

MY NOTES

7. What steps can you take to ensure that you break any negative patterns from your upbringing and foster healthier relationships in your adult life?

MY NOTES

8. Are there any aspects of the parenting style you experienced that you appreciate and want to carry forward in your own relationships or parenting approach?

MY NOTES

9. How can you use your understanding of different parenting styles to empathize with others who may have had different upbringings and experiences?

MY NOTES

MY NOTES

COMMUNICATION

Couples would benefit from learning how to communicate their thoughts and feelings in a respectful and effective manner. This means practicing active listening, where each partner listens to what the other person is saying without interrupting or jumping to conclusions. Couples should also take time to ask questions and clarify any misunderstandings before responding with their own opinions or emotions. It's also important to give each other space to express their thoughts and feelings without judgment or criticism.

Couples should be willing to compromise when needed to come up with solutions that work for everyone involved. Additionally, couples can seek out counseling or communication workshops as a means of improving their conversation skills and strengthening their relationship.

Specific steps to effectively actively listen to your partner.

1. Make eye contact and don't interrupt when your partner is speaking (I'm working on this right now- not going super well)

2. Take time to process what was said before responding with your own opinions or emotions.

3. Paraphrase and repeat back what you heard from your partner in order to make sure you both are on the same page.

4. Ask questions and clarify any misunderstandings before continuing the conversation.

5. Validate your partner's emotions without passing judgment or getting caught up in an argument.

6. Remain open-minded and be willing to compromise if needed.

7. Give each other time and space when feelings are running high while still being willing to discuss difficult topics.

8. Remain patient and understanding, even when the conversation gets heated.

9. Speak calmly and clearly, using "I" statements instead of accusing your partner of wrongdoing or making demands.

10. Show empathy towards your partner's thoughts and feelings while still holding space for your own needs.

11. Listen without distractions such as phones, TV, or other people.

12. Respect each other's boundaries and remember to keep the conversation focused on resolving the issue at hand, not attacking each other's character.

13. End the conversation with a positive statement that shows appreciation for your partner's perspective.

14. Avoid using threatening language or ultimatums that can lead to further conflict.

15. Acknowledge any progress you've made or compromises you have come to, no matter how small they may seem.

Overall, actively listening to your partner is a crucial part of communication and can help build a healthy and lasting relationship. By taking the time to really listen, couples can foster understanding and come up with solutions that work for everyone involved.

How can you make sure that both parties feel heard and respected in a conversation?

MY NOTES

How do you think taking the time to listen carefully could benefit your relationship?

MY NOTES

GENERAL TYPES OF COMMUNICATION:

1. **Verbal communication** – speaking with one another

2. **Non-verbal communication** – using body language and facial expressions to convey messages; facial expressions, and other non-spoken forms of expression

3. **Written communication** – sending messages via text, email, or other written correspondence

4. **Listening** – actively listening and understanding what someone is saying, repeating back what the other person has said to make sure that it was fully understood

5. **Empathy** – being able to understand and relate to someone else's feelings

6. **Assertiveness** – expressing your needs in a direct, respectful manner

7. **Conflict resolution** – utilizing-solving techniques when disagreements.

8. **Compromise** – finding solutions that are beneficial for both people involved in the conversation

9. **Questioning** – asking questions to gain clarity and understanding

10. **Negotiation** – coming up with solutions that meet both people's needs in a fair way.

None of these types of communication can exist without the other, so it is important for couples to understand how each one works together to create an effective conversation. By mastering the different types of communication, couples can create strong foundations for healthy and lasting relationships.

Understanding different types of communication and how it impacts relationships is important because it enables couples to learn how to communicate effectively with one another. It helps them understand each other's perspectives and feelings, as well as develop better listening skills and understanding. Knowing the various types of communication can help partners avoid unnecessary misunderstandings, improve their conflict resolution skills, and create a stronger bond. Furthermore, understanding different types of communication can also help couples come up with creative solutions to any issues that may arise in the relationship. Ultimately, it allows them to build strong foundations for their relationship and make it last longer.

Passive, aggressive, and assertive communication are all different types of verbal communication.

<u>Passive communication</u> is when someone avoids expressing their thoughts or feelings to avoid conflict. It's when one person avoids speaking up for themselves or conveying their opinions in a conversation.

Example:

Person A: "Where do you want to go for dinner?"

Person B: "Oh, I don't know. Whatever you want is fine."

Person A: "How about Italian?"

Person B: "I don't really like Italian, but it's fine."

<u>Aggressive communication</u> is when someone expresses themselves in a hostile manner, often using raised voices and insults. It's a type of verbal communication when someone is attempting to overpower the other person in the conversation. This form of communication expression is in a hostile or demeaning way and that can be damaging to relationships.

Example

Person A: "We're going to the movies tonight."

Person B: "I don't want to go to the movies tonight."

Person A: "Well, too bad. We're going anyway. Stop being so difficult and just do what I want for once."

Assertive communication is when someone expresses themselves directly and confidently without attacking or avoiding the issue. This type of communication allows someone the ability to express their needs, feelings, and opinions in a respectful manner without aggression or passivity. This type of communication allows for open dialogue that fosters understanding between partners, friends, and family members and can lead to healthier relationships.

Example:

Person A: "Where do you want to go for dinner?"

Person B: "I have a craving for sushi, but I'm open to other options. What do you think?"

Person A: "Sushi sounds great to me. Let's try that new Japanese place down the street."

Assertive communication is the most effective way of communicating in a relationship because it allows all those in a relationship with others to express their opinions while still respecting one another. So, it's the non-asshole approach. It is important for couples, friends, and family to understand the differences between these three types of verbal communication as well as non-verbal communication in order to foster a healthy and successful relationship. Non-verbal communication includes facial expressions, body language, eye contact, and more. Understanding both verbal and non-verbal communication is key to creating a successful conversation and relationship.

By understanding different types of communication and using them effectively, couples can create strong foundations for healthy relationships. It is important to remember that communication involves both verbal and non-verbal methods to ensure clear understanding. With effective communication skills, couples can foster better relationships with each other and build lasting bonds.

10 Tips on Improving Your Ability to Communicate

1. Practice active listening – listen to understand, not to respond

2. Ask questions – ask open-ended questions to gain clarity and understanding

3. Use "I" statements – be clear about your needs without blaming or attacking the other person

4. Speak honestly – say what you mean and mean what you say

5. Respect boundaries – respect yourself and your partner's feelings and needs

6. Be open to feedback – listen to constructive criticism in order to grow

7. Take timeouts – if a conversation becomes heated, take a break to cool down

8. Acknowledge emotions – validate someone else's feelings without judgment

9. Practice empathy – try to put yourself in the other person's shoes

10. Focus on solutions – come up with solutions that work for both people involved in the conversation.

Conflict resolution is the process of finding a peaceful and mutually beneficial solution to a disagreement or problem. It's important to use conflict resolution in any relationship, whether it's romantic or otherwise because it promotes communication. Conflict resolution encourages open and honest communication between individuals. It allows each person to express their feelings and opinions in a safe and respectful environment. It breaks down barriers within a relationship. Conflict can create barriers between individuals and groups.

Conflict resolution helps to break down those barriers and build stronger relationships. Through conflict resolution, individuals can gain a deeper understanding of each other's perspectives, needs, and goals. This can lead to stronger relationships and greater connections. Individuals can learn from their mistakes and grow as individuals. It encourages problem-solving and critical thinking skills. It prevents further conflict within any relationship. By finding a peaceful solution to a disagreement or problem, conflict resolution can prevent future conflicts from arising.

In any relationship, conflict is inevitable. However, it's

important to approach conflict in a healthy and productive manner. Conflict resolution promotes healthy communication, understanding, and growth.

A little ditty

Oh Communication my dear old friend how you evade me
How I wish my dyslexic brain didn't like to
play hide and seek with you

A little ditty

Through laughter and tears, we convey,
The feelings that words cannot say.
In silence, in gestures, we find,
The language that speaks to our mind.

Communication shines like a light,
Guiding us through the darkest night,

Listen and speak with your soul,
For love's true story to unfold.
With open hearts, let us share,

SETTING GROUND RULES FOR COMMUNICATION

1. Respect: The foundation of all healthy communication is respect. All parties involved must agree to treat each other with respect and not be disrespectful or demeaning in any way.

2. Eye contact: When speaking, be sure to make eye contact with the person you are talking to. This shows that you are engaged and interested in what they are saying.

3. Listen: Active listening is key when communicating effectively, meaning that you be paying close attention to the other person and not just waiting for your turn to speak.

4. No Judgement: Everyone has their own perspective, so it's important to accept different points of view without judgment or criticism.

5. Honesty: Openness and honesty are essential for building trust and fostering meaningful communication.

6. Clarity: Make sure that everyone's expectations are clear and use language that is easy to understand. Creating ground rules for communication is essential for fostering healthy relationships.

7. Respect and eye contact are key components of effective communication. Listen carefully, without judgment or criticism, and be open and honest with one another.

Make sure expectations are clear so that everyone is on the same page, and use language that can be easily understood by all parties involved. But keep in mind that you are human, so you will not do all the above 7 steps perfectly or the same way every time; I personally struggle with number 2 and 4 – these are the areas that I am working on. These are more of a guideline to help you and your person come up with rules that work for your relationship- so take what I've suggested and modify to however it best meets your needs.

What are some ways you can show empathy towards your partner's thoughts and feelings?

MY NOTES

Why is it important to remain open minded and willing to compromise when in a conversation with your partner?

MY NOTES

Communication is key in any relationship – so it's important to cultivate a space in which both people feel comfortable expressing themselves. By taking the time to learn how to communicate effectively, couples can foster a healthy and lasting connection.

ACTIVE LISTENING

By implementing active listening skills, being honest and transparent with yourself and others, setting boundaries and expectations, as well as taking responsibility for your well-being, you can create meaningful relationships that are positive and supportive. Reflecting on these points can help you gain insight into your relationships with yourself and others, as well as what is important to you in a relationship.

It also enables you to create meaningful connections by taking responsibility for your well-being, communicating openly and respectfully, and understanding when it is time to take a step back. Investing in yourself and those around you and taking the time to practice these tips will help ensure that your relationships are successful and fulfilling.

Active listening is a technique that involves entirely focusing on the person speaking, understanding their perspective, and responding thoughtfully to what they are saying.

Here are some ways to practice active listening:

Be Present: Give the speaker your full attention. Make eye contact, put away distractions (such as phones), and avoid interrupting. (Such a hard thing to do with ADHD and the anxiety around thinking you will forget what you want to say if you don't interrupt – I have found having paper with to take notes helps me in these situations and stops me from interrupting too much)

Make Observations: Observe the speaker's body language, tone, and emotional cues. This can help you better understand their perspective.

Ask Clarifying Questions: If you're unsure of something, ask clarifying questions to get a better understanding of the speaker's viewpoint. This shows that you're actively trying to understand their perspective.

Paraphrase: Repeat what the speaker said in your own words. This demonstrates that you've understood their point and gives the speaker an opportunity to clarify or expand on their thoughts.

Practice Empathy: Try to view the situation from the speaker's perspective. Put yourself in their shoes and imagine how you would feel or respond to their problem.

By actively listening, you not only gain a better

understanding of the other person, but you also show respect for their thoughts and feelings. Active listening can lead to more productive and positive communication as well as more important and meaningful relationships.

What could be some of the positive outcomes from practicing active listening with your partner?

MY NOTES

How do you think actively listening to your partner can help strengthen your relationship?

MY NOTES

What are some of the challenges you may face when trying to actively listen to your partner?

MY NOTES

What tips would you give someone who is trying to learn how to actively listen to their partner?

MY NOTES

What positive changes can you make in your relationship by actively listening to your partner?

MY NOTES

What could be some potential drawbacks of not actively listening to your partner?

MY NOTES

What are some of the steps you can take to practice active listening in a conversation with your partner?

MY NOTES

In what ways can actively listening to your partner help resolve conflicts?

MY NOTES

RULES TO FIGHT FAIR

When providing individual therapy, there comes a point in most sessions where a conversation around the person's relationships comes up, whether with a significant other or friend, or family member. I generally ask the same question during this point; do you and so and so have rules so that you fight fair? I also generally get a weird look at this point in time too. It's important, though; unless one can read minds, you do not know what is considered respectful or disrespectful in a fight/argument unless you have that conversation.

A relationship needs rules to communicate to ensure that both parties involved understand each other's expectations and boundaries. Rules provide structure, clarity, and understanding within a relationship and are essential for successful communication. They help establish trust between two people by setting out clear guidelines on how to interact with one another. Additionally, having rules in place can prevent disagreements, misunderstandings, and hurt feelings. Rules also provide stability, which is key for any relationship to thrive. Establishing a set of rules that both parties agree on will help create an atmosphere of respect and understanding. This, in turn, can lead to healthier relationships that are built on trust and mutual understanding.

Here are some fair rules to have when having a disagreement with a spouse or significant other:

1. Respect each other's opinions: It's okay to have differing opinions, but it's important to respect each other's viewpoints. In any disagreement, both sides should be able to express themselves without feeling judged or attacked.

2. Please avoid personal attacks: No matter how upset either of you may feel, it's important to avoid making personal attacks. Stick to discussing the issue at hand and avoid any criticism or harmful remarks about each other.

3. Take turns speaking: Communication is key in any relationship, but it's just as important to listen. Take turns speaking and actively listen to your spouse without interrupting so that both parties have a chance to express themselves. (I suck at this one – and I'm a therapist!)

4. Focus on the issue, not the person: During the

disagreement, make sure to keep the focus on the issue at hand, not on the person. Remember that the disagreement is not a reflection of your overall relationship.

5. Use "I" statements: Communicate how you feel using "I" statements instead of "you" statements. This helps prevent the other person from feeling blamed, judged or attacked. (hmm, that sounds familiar)

6. Take a break if needed: If the disagreement becomes heated or emotionally overwhelming, it's okay to take a break and come back to it later. This allows space for both parties to cool down and resume the conversation with a clearer head.

By establishing these fair rules in a disagreement with your spouse, you can promote a respectful and healthy dialogue that leads to a stronger relationship. Please add on or change the rules to meet your and your partner's needs.

Why is it important to give each other time and space when feelings are running high, while still being willing to discuss difficult topics?

MY NOTES

MY NOTES

What are some things you can do to make sure the conversation remains healthy and productive?

MY NOTES

How can you ensure that both sides of a conversation are taken into consideration when discussing an issue?

MY NOTES

What specific communication skills have you learned or improved in your current relationships?

MY NOTES

MY NOTES

What are some strategies you can use to ensure that conversations remain respectful and constructive?

MY NOTES

How do you foster a safe space for yourself and your partner(s) to share their thoughts and feelings without judgment?

MY NOTES

What have been some of the most difficult conversations you've had in relationships?

MY NOTES

How can couples work together to come up with compromises that benefit both parties equally?

MY NOTES

In what ways could you be more mindful and patient when communicating with your partner(s)?

MY NOTES

What are some positive things that have come out of difficult conversations?

MY NOTES

How can you continue to work on improving your communication skills in relationships?

MY NOTES

What do you think is the most important thing to remember when having a conversation with someone about their thoughts and feelings?

MY NOTES

How has effective communication skills helped to build strong, healthy relationships in your life?

MY NOTES

STORY TIME

Once upon a time, there were two best friends, a cat named Alex and a dog named Emma. They lived together in harmony until, one day, they got into a fight over who got to play with the squeaky toy. Alex swatted Emma's nose with her paw, causing the toy to fly across the room and hit the lamp, breaking it. Emma was furious.

"That was my favorite toy!" she barked. Alex wasn't happy either. "Well, you're always hogging it. It's my turn to play with it."

The two of them started to argue, hissing, and barking, until they realized they needed conflict resolution. So they took a deep breath and sat down to talk it through.

After a few minutes of discussion, they decided to create a schedule. Alex would get the toy on Mondays, Wednesdays, and Fridays, and Emma would get it on Tuesdays, Thursdays, and Saturdays. On Sundays, they would take turns.

It wasn't a perfect solution, but it was a fair compromise. Plus, they realized that they had been taking their friendship for granted and didn't want to lose it over a silly toy.

So the two of them snuggled up together, with the squeaky toy between them, and lived happily ever after - at least until the next time they fought over something.

But they knew they could always use conflict resolution to work things out.

How lovely it would be if conflict resolution was as simple as the story made it out to be.

WTF IS THE 100% RULE?

The 100/0 principle was developed by Al Ritter, a motivational speaker and author of the book "The 100/0 Principle: The Secret of Great Relationships." Ritter developed the concept as a way to help people improve their relationships with others, both personally and professionally.

According to Ritter, the idea behind the 100/0 principle is that taking full responsibility for a relationship, without expecting anything in return, can lead to greater happiness, success, and fulfillment. By giving without expectation, we can eliminate the potential for disappointment or resentment, which can damage relationships over time.

Ritter believes that the 100/0 principle is particularly important in today's fast-paced, technology-driven world, where people often feel disconnected from one another. By committing to the relationship and giving our all, even when it's difficult or inconvenient, we can build stronger, more meaningful connections with the people in our lives.

Overall, the 100/0 principle is a simple but powerful concept that encourages people to take ownership of their relationships and commit to giving their best in every interaction.

The 100/0 principle is a concept that involves taking full responsibility for a relationship without expecting anything in return. It requires a strong commitment to the relationship and the self-discipline to give your all, regardless of the other person's actions or behavior.

Implementing the 100/0 principle can be challenging, as it goes against our natural tendencies to expect reciprocity in our relationships. However, it can be incredibly beneficial for both parties involved. By taking full responsibility for the relationship, you empower yourself to make positive changes and create a stronger, healthier bond with the other person. Additionally, by giving without expecting anything in return, you eliminate the potential for disappointment or resentment, which can damage relationships over time.

To implement the 100/0 principle, start by focusing on your own thoughts and behaviors. Make a conscious effort to give 100% in every interaction, regardless of how the other person responds. This may involve being more patient, attentive, and empathetic, even when you're upset or frustrated. Remember that taking responsibility for the relationship means taking ownership of your own feelings and actions, rather than blaming the other person for any issues that arise.

Another way to implement the 100/0 principle is to practice gratitude. Instead of focusing on what you're not getting from the other person, focus on what you appreciate about them. This can help you shift from a mindset of expectation to one of appreciation, which can strengthen your relationship and help you feel more fulfilled.

Finally, it's important to communicate openly and honestly with the other person. Let them know that you're committed to the relationship and that you're willing to put in the effort to make it work. Be clear about your expectations and boundaries, but also be open to listening to their perspective and working together to find solutions that benefit both of you.

Remember that implementing the 100/0 principle takes time and effort, but it can have significant benefits for your relationships and overall well-being. By taking responsibility for the relationship and giving without expectation, you can create a stronger, more fulfilling bond with the people in your life.

STORY TIME

Once upon a time, in the quaint town of Twin Forks, lived two best friends named Emma and Alex. They were inseparable and had been friends since childhood. They shared many adventures together, but as they grew older, their friendship was put to the test.

One sunny day, Emma and Alex decided to start a lemonade stand together. They agreed to split the profits equally and worked tirelessly to set up their stand. However, things didn't go as smoothly as they had hoped.

Emma, believing in the 100/0 rule, took full responsibility for the lemonade stand without expecting anything in return from Alex. Emma woke up early every morning to make fresh lemonade, set up the stand, and greeted each customer with a warm smile. No matter how tired or frustrated Emma felt, they continued to give their all to make the lemonade stand a success.

On the other hand, Alex didn't follow the 100/0 rule. Instead, Alex expected Emma to do most of the work and only showed up when it suited them. As a result, their friendship began to suffer, and tensions rose between the two friends.

Despite the challenges, Emma's unwavering commitment to the 100/0 rule kept the lemonade stand afloat. Eventually, customers began to notice Emma's dedication and hard work, and the lemonade stand became the talk of the town. People came from far and wide to taste the delicious lemonade and experience Emma's exceptional customer service.

As the lemonade stand thrived, Alex couldn't help but feel envious of Emma's success. Alex decided to open their own lemonade stand, just a few blocks away. However, instead of following the 100/0 rule like Emma, Alex chose to focus solely on their own needs and expectations.

Alex's lemonade stand struggled to attract customers, as people preferred Emma's warm and welcoming approach. This made Alex realize the importance of the 100/0 rule and how it had positively impacted Emma's life and relationships.

Feeling remorseful, Alex approached Emma and apologized for their lack of commitment to their shared lemonade stand. Emma, being the kind-hearted person they were, forgave Alex and welcomed them back with open arms.

Together, they combined their lemonade stands and continued to practice the 100/0 rule in their friendship and business. As a result, their lemonade stand became more successful than ever before, and their bond grew stronger.

In the end, Emma and Alex learned that by taking full responsibility for their relationships and giving their all without expecting anything in return, they could overcome any obstacles and create a happier, more fulfilling life together.

And so, the two friends continued to spread the magic of the 100/0 rule throughout TwoForks, touching the hearts of everyone who tasted their delicious lemonade.

How do you currently approach your relationships? Do you tend to expect a trade-off, or do you give without expecting anything in return?

MY NOTES

What are some examples of situations where you've successfully applied the 100/0 principle in your relationships? How did it impact those relationships?

MY NOTES

Can you identify any relationships in your life that could benefit from implementing the 100/0 principle? What specific actions can you take to apply this rule in those relationships?

MY NOTES

How do you think the 100/0 principle might help you overcome any challenges or obstacles you're facing in your current relationships?

MY NOTES

In what ways can practicing the 100/0 principle help you grow as an individual and improve your overall well-being?

MY NOTES

How does the 100/0 rule align with your personal values and beliefs about relationships and personal responsibility?

MY NOTES

Have you ever experienced a relationship where someone else practiced the 100/0 principle towards you? How did it make you feel, and how did it impact the relationship?

MY NOTES

What strategies can you use to maintain the 100/0 mindset even during difficult or emotionally charged situations?

MY NOTES

Reflect on a time when you struggled to implement the 100/0 principle in a relationship. What were the challenges you faced, and what lessons did you learn from that experience?

MY NOTES

How can you support and encourage others in your life to practice the 100/0 rule in their own relationships?

MY NOTES

MY NOTES

EPILOGUE

I don't know about you but that was a lot of information, and I will totally have to re-read my book a couple of times and I only scratched the surface. Writing this book also made me realize how little any of these topics were ever discussed in school, on TV shows, or at dinner. You may read this and have some moments of "duh" that's common sense but why didn't I realize that in the moment? Why did it take reading a book to open my eyes to something that seems so simple? It only seems simple because you can move the lens back and take a different look. When you are in the eye of the storm, in your personal storm that encompasses you, friends, family, social environment, etc. You can't see past the storm; you are unable to see the larger picture. One is not able to take that look and see the entirety of what's going on they can't ever get that perspective for themselves because they're in the eye of the storm, so reading this forces you to get that different perspective that you would not have had otherwise. So, you may have a moment where it's like oh Duh! why didn't I think of that or that's that just common sense again? You can't have these thoughts for yourself because you're in the middle of it I can't do it for myself you can't do it for yourself that's why it's important to seek out books and podcasts and coaches and therapists and friends that challenge you - that have you looking at the world differently. That's the beauty of having a relationship.

Relationships: healthy ones can give us back that outside perspective that we might not otherwise be able to access. I don't know about you, but I grew up in the late 80s and early 90s; the complexities of relationships did not show up on "Jem", "She-Ra", Saved by the Bell" maybe on "Blossom" but my parents did not let me watch that due to it being "too mature". The relationships that I saw for whatever reason didn't seem to work out; Jem always lied to her boyfriend about what she did for a living, Rainbow Brite didn't seem to have any stable relationships and as I got older well "Friends: was unrealistic to me, "Sabrina" didn't really explain boundaries she just used her magic when she needed a break. That weird "Dinosaurs" are not exactly role models for relationships.

Of course, I had my parents as real living models, but what

preteen or teen really pays that much attention to their parents? My large catholic southside dysfunctional family; well let's just say there is a reason I'm a therapist. Again, I digress; my point is that this may sound like common sense but it's not; we in our society especially when I was growing up did not have these conversations in our home or in our school. No one just magically knows how to have a healthy grown-up relationship; there is a reason why our divorce rate is as high as it is. So, take the time to read, listen to pod casts, watch you tube and learn about what a healthy relationship is and the steps to keep it that way. If you wanted to fix something, you would read a manual well relationships don't come with manuals, but you can find a book or two out there to help you along your way.

AFTERWORD

What's with the Cheesy Story?

As a child I had a problem with learning how to read, my brain just could not sound spell / remember the sounds of words, etc. I had to go to tutoring in the summer, pulled out of class weekly for speech services, and get support from a special education teacher just for reading. I'm a skinny blonde with big glasses, catholic in the late 80s and I get pulled out of class for special education – let me tell you this could have gone so south but thank God for my ADHD because I was so inattentive to social cues that I didn't look at this as a bad thing. I did not have the attention span to really pick up on the fact that this was different and therefore something to be embarrassed about. Sure, it was frustrating and challenging for me, but it did not horribly scare me or negatively impact my self-worth – high school did that, no one gets out of childhood unscathed – I would be unemployed. ADHD saved the day. Who knew that being oblivious to the world around me could be the very thing at saved me at such a young age.

I digress though; I learned that for me to retain the information I needed to chunk it up, write it down, create notes, and find different ways to retain it. So, I naturally write that way; I include breaks for my brain and ways to force myself to pause. A book with anecdotes and checklists can make it easier to retain information because it engages multiple parts of our brains. The anecdotes help us connect new information to existing memories and make it more relatable and interesting. Meanwhile, the checklists provide a structured framework to organize and categorize the information, making it easier to understand and remember.

Additionally, having a physical book with tangible pages that we can touch, write on and highlight can also aid in retention. Studies have shown that people tend to retain information better when they read it in print rather than on a screen.

By combining anecdotes with checklists in a book format, we activate both sides of our brain, enhance our memory capacity, and produce a more comprehensive and engaging learning experience. I like to use techniques and tricks that work; time is so valuable to me due to how much extra time and energy I must put into reading and writing due to my dyslexia and ADHD. My books will include areas to write and checklists and stories and at times may seem silly or childish, but you will remember my story or checklist, won't you?

ABOUT THE AUTHOR

Erin Vandermore

Erin Vandermore, LCMHC-S, LCPC currently resides in the picturesque mountains of Asheville North Carolina. Erin has been married to her partner for 16 years and is the mother of 2 wonderful children. She is a pre-eclampsia survivor, a person living with Dyslexia, ADHD and Anxiety. As if her wife and 2 children were  not a big enough challenge to her patience, she also owns 3 semi-trained dogs, 2 of which have anxiety issues and one with bladder control problems. In her free time…. Who are we kidding? She has no free time. However, on the rare occasions when Erin manages to escape from the insanity of her daily life, she enjoys floating down the French Broad River with her family and fantasizing about being shipwrecked on an island.

Made in the USA
Columbia, SC
02 October 2024